Workbook for Dr. Nicole LePera's
How to Be the Love You Seek

Exercises for Reflection and Processing the Lessons

 **BIG ACTION BOOKS**

BigActionBooks.com

Contents

Claim your free bonus

There's a free bonus waiting for you as thanks for picking up this workbook. We think you'll like it. Inside, you'll find a list of the most impactful self development books from this year, including:
- Top books for self-growth and mindfulness
- Top books for financial growth
- Top books for relationships (including yourself)
- Top books for productivity and "Getting Things Done"

We hope they provide a little inspiration for you - and perhaps some new discoveries.

To get your free bonus, scan the QR code below or visit BigActionBooks.com/bonus.

Scan to get your free bonus

Introduction

Strengthen your relationships by tapping into the power of the heart.

WHY THIS WORKBOOK?

You've read Dr. Nicole LePera's fabulous book about creating deeper and more harmonious connections with others by accessing the potential of the heart. Now it's time to actually *practice* it - write; journal; put the lessons in motion.

This workbook was created as a **companion** to Dr. Nicole LePera's "How to Be the Love You Seek". While reading the book, we found ourselves wishing for a place where we could write, process and practise the book's exercises in a constructive, concise way. The exercises are excellent - but there isn't much space to actually write in the book itself. Instead, we found ourselves cobbling them together in various places - notebooks, journals, pieces of paper - all of which would eventually get lost, or at the very least, not be helpful in putting the lessons into practice. That's how this workbook was born.

HOW TO USE THIS WORKBOOK

This workbook is like a faithful friend to How to Be the Love You Seek. In it, you'll find exactly what's advertised: the exercises from the book, summarised and formatted, with space to answer.

- All exercises from How to Be the Love You Seek, extracted into one single place
- Space to write under each exercise
- Lists, ruled lines and space for you to answer, journal and reflect
- Clearly organised and well-formatted so it's easy to follow

In each section, we've extracted the main premise of the exercise, and then added space to respond and practise the lessons. This may come in the format of a table to fill in, space to free-write, or other exercise methods to provide space for reflection. You'll also notice the "Parts" and "Chapters" referenced in the book, so you can easily find the section if you need to look back on it for further context.

If you want to not only read about how to strengthen self-love and transform relationships. - but also put the lessons into practice - this workbook, as well as your own dedication, will help you do just that.

Enjoy, and thank you.
Let's dive in!

---

* Please note: This is an unofficial workbook companion for How to Be the Love You Seek to help motivated do-ers process the lessons from this fantastic book. It is not created by or associated with the author in any official way.

How to use this workbook: Our goal in this workbook is to 'bring to the surface' some of the relationship dynamics we experience now, or have experienced in the past. To better understand ourselves, be more mindful, and therefore be in a better position to adjust and change them.

With this in mind, try to reserve judgement here and be kind to yourself as well as the other people that come up. This applies to exercise below, and, indeed, to all exercises within the workbook. Try not to 'judge' your answers here, and simply note down what comes up.

You can cross-reference the exercises in this workbook, with the chapters in the original book. You'll find them below in that order, with space to write underneath each one.

There's also a section at the back of this notebook for free-form notes and journaling. With that - let's go!

CHAPTER 1: The Power of Your Relationships

Checklist: Your Emotional Safety and Security

Pause and reflect on your connections with your parental figures or early caregivers. Reflecting on the below, select the ones that most accurately describe your childhood experiences in a consistent way.

Note: Throughout this workbook, you'll see examples in some places, listed in *grey handwriting like this*. These are just to give you an idea of the kind of action points you might like to take - but feel free to use or ignore them as best suits your style. There's also a section at the back of this notebook for free-form notes and journaling.

- ☐ I received comfort and support from adults who were emotionally available when I felt upset.
- ☐ I observed adults establishing boundaries and effectively communicating their limits without resorting to abusive discipline or intimidating threats.
- ☐ I had the freedom to explore age-appropriate behaviours without being burdened with adult responsibilities, such as counselling their emotions, caring for younger siblings, or being used as a tool for manipulation or control.
- ☐ I learned safe ways to express my feelings through the example of adults who didn't dominate the emotional atmosphere at home with their own emotions. They regularly asked about my feelings, and validated our shared emotional experiences.
- ☐ I saw adults demonstrating how to communicate emotional needs directly, seeking support without resorting to manipulative tactics like the silent treatment, rage, guilt-tripping, shaming, or blaming.

☐ I witnessed adults consistently taking responsibility for their actions and offering apologies for their role in conflicts and emotional upsets.

☐ I was given the freedom to develop my individuality by adults who allowed me to explore my own ideas and thoughts, without pressuring me to conform to others' beliefs or succumb to groupthink.

☐ I was actively encouraged to pursue my curiosities and passions by adults who asked questions and expressed a genuine interest in knowing more.

The higher the number of boxes you marked, the greater the chance that you enjoyed stable and protected relationships during your upbringing. Conversely, if, similar to the author situation, you find it challenging to some or many of the childhood experiences above, it suggests that your early relationships probably didn't offer the safety and assurance necessary for you to deepen your emotional expression. But here's the good news: the techniques presented in the book (and this workbook!) will provide you with a chance to establish a sense of safety and security independently, irrespective of your past circumstances.

Your Relationship Experiences and Beliefs Exploration

Reflect on the different connections in your life, starting with your parental figures or those who took care of you at a young age. Examine the following prompts and note down your thoughts, below.

During your childhood, how frequently (and at what times) were your needs (both physical and emotional) satisfied?

Example: Whenever I was upset after having a fight with a friend, I was always comforted by my mom.

_____

_____

_____

_____

_____

_____

During your childhood, how frequently (and at what times) did **your needs go unmet**, whether they were physical or emotional?

_____

_____

_____

_____

_____

_____

During your childhood, how frequently (and at what times) were you required to **oversee or attend to the needs (both physical and emotional) of others**, including your parental figures or those looking after you?

_____

_____

_____

_____

_____

_____

_____

_____

During your childhood, how frequently (and at what times) did you **seek out your parents or other caregivers for safety or for protection and comfort**, leading to a sense of trust in others and the world around you?

_____

_____

_____

_____

_____

During your childhood, how frequently (and at what times) did you experience **an urge to escape from those who played parental roles in your life, in order to seek safety or provide comfort for yourself**? Consequently, you may have developed a tendency to feel apprehensive about others, or the surrounding world.

_____

_____

_____

_____

_____

_____

During your childhood, how frequently (and at what times) did you **feel joy or pleasure?**

_____

_____

_____

_____

_____

_____

_____

_____

During your childhood, how frequently (and at what times) did you encounter **feelings of spontaneity or playfulness?**

_____

_____

_____

_____

_____

_____

_____

_____

During your childhood, how frequently (and at what times) did your parents or other caregivers demonstrate **negotiation and cooperative approaches to problem-solving**?

_____

_____

_____

_____

_____

_____

Next, take a moment to reflect on your **adult relationships**. Delve into the questions below and note down your thoughts.

When it comes to **relationships,** *I think...*

_____

_____

_____

_____

When **love** comes to mind, *I think...*

_____

_____

_____

_____

When it comes to **relationships, *I feel...***

_____

_____

_____

_____

_____

_____

When **love** comes to mind, ***I feel...***

_____

_____

_____

_____

_____

CHAPTER 2: Exploring Your Embodied Self

Checklist: Your Authentic Needs

Many of us are out of touch with our physical, emotional, and spiritual needs due to the influences of our upbringing. As such, it's crucial to identify the needs that are currently unmet. Pause for a while to examine the following checklist - aim to be sincere and impartial as you consider the following prompts, and check the response(s) that best mirror your present reality:

AM I PROVIDING MY BODY WITH THE ESSENTIAL NUTRIENTS IT NEEDS?

☐ I pay attention to my body, having a meal when it signals hunger and stopping it's when satisfied.

☐ I opt for foods that provide a sense of fullness and energy (whenever possible).

☐ I recognize the foods that bring lethargy, restlessness, or general discomfort, and steer clear of them (when feasible).

☐ I usually experience mental alertness and clarity.

DO I ENGAGE IN PHYSICAL ACTIVITY?

☐ I move my body every day, whether in an intense way or at a slower pace.

☐ I recognize when my body needs a break or some rest, and I give myself that.

☐ I can feel of my muscles tensing up and loosening.

☐ I observe changes in my body and how its energy shifts when I engage in movement versus when I don't.

DO I PROVIDE ADEQUATE REST FOR MY BODY?

☐ I quickly drift into sleep once I get into bed.

☐ I can maintain uninterrupted sleep throughout the night (or if I do wake up, I can return to sleep quickly and easily).

☐ When I wake up, I feel revitalized and reenergized.

☐ I notice the impact of insufficient sleep on my mood and behavior.

CAN I HANDLE STRESS?

☐ I recognize the influence of the people around me on my stress levels.

☐ I acknowledge the effect of the information I engage with (social media, news, entertainment) on my stress levels.

☐ I can identify when stress is affecting me, and try to self-soothe when feasible.

☐ I incorporate moments of solitude, quiet, silence, or connection with nature into my daily routine.

AM I EMOTIONALLY AT EASE AND PROTECTED?

- ☐ I have a sense of safety and freedom to express my true self in my relationships.
- ☐ I know what interests me and what I'm passionate about.
- ☐ I welcome new experiences and create time to delve into my creativity.
- ☐ I carve out space for impromptu, lighthearted, or unstructured time in my day.

Be kind to yourself, and show compassion if you haven't been able to answer 'yes' to a lot of the answers mentioned earlier. The upcoming exercises in this workbook (as well as the original book), will discuss methods to start addressing these fundamental needs and mend your connection with your body.

Notes/insights on the above:

_____

_____

_____

_____

_____

Body Consciousness Check-in

To cultivate awareness of your body, consider incorporating moments of body consciousness into your daily routine. Integrating these pauses into your day can redirect your focus away from an overly active thinking mind, allowing you to practice tuning in to your body's present-moment sensations. By first checking in with your body before engaging in any physical self-care activities, such as eating, resting, or moving, you'll enhance your connection to your body and its diverse physical needs. Setting alarms at intervals during the day can serve as reminders to pause and attend to your physical well-being. During these moments, shift your attention entirely to the sensations within your body.

Below, note down and reflect on your experiences as you start this practice. In this workbook, we've created space for 3 check-ins per day over 7 days as you being to incorporate this into your daily routine.

Daily Consciousness Check-ins

Day #1

Body pause: [time] ___*9:00 AM*_____

Physical sensations present:

Example: Faster heartbeat and tense muscles from doing morning exercise.

_____

_____

_____

_____

Body pause: [time] _____

Physical sensations present:

_____

_____

_____

_____

Body pause: [time] _____

Physical sensations present:

_____

_____

_____

_____

Day #2
Body pause: [time] _____
Physical sensations present:

_____

_____

_____

_____

Body pause: [time] _____
Physical sensations present:

_____

_____

_____

_____

Body pause: [time] _____
Physical sensations present:

_____

_____

_____

_____

Day #3

Body pause: [time] _____

Physical sensations present:

_____

_____

_____

_____

Body pause: [time] _____

Physical sensations present:

_____

_____

_____

_____

Body pause: [time] _____

Physical sensations present:

_____

_____

_____

_____

Day #4

Body pause: [time] _____
Physical sensations present:

_____

_____

_____

_____

Body pause: [time] _____
Physical sensations present:

_____

_____

_____

_____

Body pause: [time] _____
Physical sensations present:

_____

_____

_____

_____

Day #5

Body pause: [time] _____

Physical sensations present:

_____

_____

_____

_____

Body pause: [time] _____

Physical sensations present:

_____

_____

_____

_____

Body pause: [time] _____

Physical sensations present:

_____

_____

_____

_____

Day #6
Body pause: [time] _____
Physical sensations present:

_____

_____

_____

_____

Body pause: [time] _____
Physical sensations present:

_____

_____

_____

_____

Body pause: [time] _____
Physical sensations present:

_____

_____

_____

_____

Day #7

Body pause: [time] _____

Physical sensations present:

_____

_____

_____

_____

Body pause: [time] _____

Physical sensations present:

_____

_____

_____

_____

Body pause: [time] _____

Physical sensations present:

_____

_____

_____

_____

Notes/insights on this exercise:

_____

_____

_____

_____

_____

Consciousness Check-in

As you might be realizing, consciousness plays a crucial role in our journey to embody our true self. The author notes that to enhance her cognitive awareness, or her capacity to observe my subconscious patterns, she established a practice she calls the daily consciousness check-in. This method helps bring awareness to the things that happen automatically in your life. It's important to be patient with yourself during the initial stages of this practice. Because our brain tends to operate on autopilot to conserve energy, transitioning into a conscious state of awareness can feel physically draining.

The steps involved in a consciousness check-in mirror the steps we saw above in a body consciousness pause. Begin by setting an intention to pause three times a day to observe or recognize two things: your current <u>activity </u>and where your <u>attention</u> lies in that moment.

Here are two effective ways to establish your new daily check-in routine. You can use either approach as you work on solidifying these daily intentions, until check-ins become second nature or until you naturally remember to pause for moments of consciousness throughout the day:

1. Set an intention to check in at three specific times during the day, such as 11:00 a.m., 4:00 p.m., and 9:00 p.m. You may consider setting an alarm or using your phone to remind you.

2. Set an intention to check in during three routine daily activities, such as enjoying your morning coffee, preparing your post-work meal, and getting ready for bed.

During the check-in, ask yourself the following two questions:

1. What am I **currently doing** (washing the dishes, watching a TV show, talking with someone)?

2. Where is my **attention**? Am I fully immersed in my current activity or conversation, or am I lost in thoughts about other things? If it's the latter, what occupies my thoughts (e.g., a conversation from earlier, a recent credit card statement, an upcoming event, a work-related stressor)?

Your objective during this practice is simply to be present in the moment, observing your thoughts like clouds drifting across the sky. You can use the following prompts to note down your responses ro the two check-in points.

Similar to the previous exercise, below in this workbook is space to do this for 7 days as you start to establish this daily practice.

Daily Consciousness Check-ins

Day 1:
Check-in #1
1. What am I currently **doing**?

_____

2. Where is my **attention directed**? Am I fully immersed in my current activity or conversation, or am I lost in thoughts about other matters? If the latter, what occupies my thoughts?

_____

_____

Check-in #2
1. What am I **currently doing**?

_____

2. Where is my **attention directed**?

_____

_____

Check-in #3
1. What am I **currently doing**?

_____

2. Where is my **attention directed**?

_____

_____

Day 2:

Check-in #1

1. What am I currently **doing**?

_____

2. Where is my **attention directed**? Am I fully immersed in my current activity or conversation, or am I lost in thoughts about other matters? If the latter, what occupies my thoughts?

_____

_____

Check-in #2

1. What am I **currently doing**?

_____

2. Where is my **attention directed**?

_____

_____

Check-in #3

1. What am I **currently doing**?

_____

2. Where is my **attention directed**?

_____

_____

Day 3:

Check-in #1

1. What am I currently **doing**?

_____

2. Where is my **attention directed**? Am I fully immersed in my current activity or conversation, or am I lost in thoughts about other matters? If the latter, what occupies my thoughts?

_____

_____

Check-in #2

1. What am I **currently doing**?

_____

2. Where is my **attention directed**?

_____

_____

Check-in #3

1. What am I **currently doing**?

_____

2. Where is my **attention directed**?

_____

_____

Day 4:

Check-in #1

1. What am I currently **doing**?

_____

2. Where is my **attention directed**? Am I fully immersed in my current activity or conversation, or am I lost in thoughts about other matters? If the latter, what occupies my thoughts?

_____

_____

Check-in #2

1. What am I **currently doing**?

_____

2. Where is my **attention directed**?

_____

_____

Check-in #3

1. What am I **currently doing**?

_____

2. Where is my **attention directed**?

_____

_____

Day 5:

Check-in #1

1. What am I currently **doing**?

_____

2. Where is my **attention directed**? Am I fully immersed in my current activity or conversation, or am I lost in thoughts about other matters? If the latter, what occupies my thoughts?

_____

_____

Check-in #2

1. What am I **currently doing**?

_____

2. Where is my **attention directed**?

_____

_____

Check-in #3

1. What am I **currently doing**?

_____

2. Where is my **attention directed**?

_____

_____

Day 6:
Check-in #1
1. What am I currently **doing**?

_____

2. Where is my **attention directed**? Am I fully immersed in my current activity or conversation, or am I lost in thoughts about other matters? If the latter, what occupies my thoughts?

_____

_____

Check-in #2
1. What am I **currently doing**?

_____

2. Where is my **attention directed**?

_____

_____

Check-in #3
1. What am I **currently doing**?

_____

2. Where is my **attention directed**?

_____

_____

Day 7:

Check-in #1

1. What am I currently **doing**?

_____

2. Where is my **attention directed**? Am I fully immersed in my current activity or conversation, or am I lost in thoughts about other matters? If the latter, what occupies my thoughts?

_____

_____

Check-in #2

1. What am I **currently doing**?

_____

2. Where is my **attention directed**?

_____

_____

Check-in #3

1. What am I **currently doing**?

_____

2. Where is my **attention directed**?

_____

_____

Come back to this tool as frequently as required. The author mentions that she still often incorporates it into her daily routine.

Notes/insights on the above:

_____

_____

_____

_____

_____

Heart Check-in

We might be aware of our likes and dislikes, but often ignore our **instinctual** needs or wishes due to fear of losing safety and connection to the world and our loved ones. To genuinely express yourself, it's beneficial to start recognizing the worries or fears that might be hindering you. Take a moment to recall a recent interaction with someone where you wanted to express yourself but refrained from voicing your genuine thoughts, emotions, or viewpoints. Now, note down your answers to these prompts:

What do I genuinely feel, think, or want to do?

_____

_____

_____

What do I worry might happen if I express my genuine thoughts and/or true feelings in this moment?

_____

_____

_____

What might I feel if I were to share my true feelings and thoughts?

_____

_____

_____

Using the probing questions and prompts in the previous group of exercises, spend some time during the coming weeks to observe yourself throughout the day and across various relationships.

Take note of any recurring patterns in instances where you find yourself holding back genuine thoughts, perspectives, or emotions. Initially, connecting with your innermost thoughts, feelings, or aspirations might prove challenging as your mind is likely preoccupied with distracting thoughts. Keep giving yourself grace and compassion, especially if introspective questioning is new to you.

Consistently take brief pauses for body awareness and periodic self-checks, taking your attentionn from the mental realm to your physical body. This shift allows for a clearer reception of your heart's messages. Regularly tuning into your heart, particularly before significant decisions, aids in the ongoing process of rebuilding your connection with your authentic self or soul.

As you gain insight into your heart's desires, have patience when articulating these authentic needs and wants to others. Start by noticing instances where you agree or say "yes" to matters that are not in line with your truth, or just aren't interesting to you. When invited to an event you have no desire to attend, don't accept straight away.

Instead, take a moment to consciously choose a response aligned with your genuine needs and wants. Throughout this self-discovery journey, remember that identifying what you really want (or don't), and what's true (or what isn't true), will ultimately guide you toward knowing genuine - and what you truly want for yourself.

Notes/insights on the above:

_____

_____

_____

_____

_____

_____

_____

_____

_____

_____

_____

_____

CHAPTER 3: Understanding the Neurobiology of Trauma Bonds

Referring to the book's checklists for the various 'modes' we might find ourselves in, use the exercises below (in conjunction with the book, if needed) to reflect on and learn about your style and what to look for.

Nervous System Checklist

ERUPTOR MODE (FIGHT RESPONSE)

I'm noticing the tendency I have, to take things personally, react defensively, control conversations, engage in arguments, experience anger or intense frustration, create lingering resentment, maintain grudges, or conjure up vendettas. I might engage in behaviors like bullying, shaming, belittling, minimizing, or adopting a highly critical and judgmental attitude towards both myself and others.

BODY:

- ☐ I have difficulty unwinding and may feel uneasy, restless, stirred up, or on anxious.
- ☐ My heartbeat speeds up.
- ☐ There's sweating or trembling in my body, and my shoulders might be squared or my chest inflated.
- ☐ I'm breathing rapidly and superficially, using my chest instead of breathing deeply from my abdomen.
- ☐ My muscles (jaw, neck, upper back) are taut, and my hands and fists are clenched.
- ☐ I'm speaking loudly, perhaps even shouting.
- ☐ My eyes are intensely focused or fixed on something or someone nearby ("tunnel vision").

MIND:

- ☐ I tend to scrutinize myself or others intensely or harshly in my thoughts.
- ☐ My thoughts tend to be deeply emotional and might get caught in extreme patterns (such as repeatedly thinking "I have completely failed" or "They are entirely wrong") in reaction to a challenging or distressing situation.

DISTRACTOR MODE (FLIGHT RESPONSE)

I'm aware that I am withdrawing into my thoughts or seeking refuge in my to-do's or agenda or by consuming food, beverages, or other substances. I divert the conversation, exit uncomfortable discussions or evade, steer clear of, or disconnect from others when I sense a potential disturbance or conflict.

BODY:

- ☐ I find it challenging to unwind and may experience discomfort, restlessness, agitation, or anxiety.
- ☐ My heartbeat speeds up.
- ☐ I sweat or shake, and my stance may be hunched (making me appear smaller) or I feel a desire to fade into the background.
- ☐ I breathe rapidly and shallowly, mainly from my chest rather than deeply from my abdomen.
- ☐ My muscles (jaw, neck, upper back) are tight and might be trembling or shaking.
- ☐ I might not be engaging in conversation, could be speaking softly, or might be babbling or attempting to change the topic of discussion.
- ☐ My gaze is unfocused, or I'm avoiding eye contact with my surroundings entirely, and my attention is directed elsewhere (such as on my phone or a TV screen).

MIND:

- ☐ My mind is in overdrive, and I might find it challenging to focus on tasks or engage in clear and critical thinking.
- ☐ My thoughts are intensely focused on a specific subject or topic.

DETACHER MODE (FREEZE or SHUTDOWN RESPONSE)

I notice myself withdrawing, disengaging, or completely disconnecting. I experience a sense of numbness or emptiness. My mind feels blank, and it's difficult to connect with my thoughts and emotions, and it's also tough to express them verbally to others.

BODY:

- [ ] I experience a sense of disconnection or indifference and may also sense feelings of sadness, hopelessness, or lack of motivation.
- [ ] My heart rate has decreased or become nearly imperceptible.
- [ ] My body might register as cold or numb, generally 'shrunken', with my head lowered.
- [ ] I'm breathing with a tight chest, perhaps even holding my breath, and experiencing an overall stiffness in my midsection.
- [ ] Overall my muscles feel weak, and this is coupled with feelings of fatigue or heaviness.
- [ ] I feel physical exhaustion, a depletion of energy, or a pervasive numbness, making it challenging to feel any emotions or physical sensations whatsoever.
- [ ] I might be silent or express myself with a flat, monotone, or c forced speech, often responding with nods or one-word answers.
- [ ] There is a blank or distant stare in my eyes.

MIND:

- [ ] I feel a sense of detachment and struggle to discern reality from imagination.
- [ ] My thoughts seem empty, and it feels hard to focus on activities or engage in clear and analytical thinking.

PLEASER MODE (FAWN RESPONSE)

I'm often focused on the well-being of others, sometimes assuming complete responsibility for predicting their needs, emotions, or behaviors. I often find myself providing too much of an explanation when it isn't needed, or over-justifying my thoughts, emotions, or decisions to others.

BODY:

- ☐ I feel out of touch with my own body and frequently struggle to recognize my emotions.
- ☐ My focus is intensely on the people or environment around me.
- ☐ I may unconsciously match my breathing to that of the people I'm with.
- ☐ My energy tends to align with the energy of those close to me, or the overall atmosphere.
- ☐ My eyes are consistently surveying someone or something in my external surroundings.

MIND:

- ☐ I'm constantly anticipating the next potential problem ("waiting for the other shoe to drop").
- ☐ I find myself worried by thoughts or anxiety about others being angry or displeased with me, or concerns about external circumstances in general.

Notes/insights on the above:

_____

_____

_____

_____

CONNECTOR MODE (SAFE AND SOCIAL RESPONSE)

I feel a sense of calm, security, and a willingness to interact or connect with people or things around me. I am curious and capable of viewing situations from new angles, making room for intricacies and contradictions, while staying rooted and adaptable to whatever happens.

BODY:

- ☐ I feel a state of physical alertness, calmn, and focused.
- ☐ My posture is open, at ease, and relaxed, with my arms casually hanging by my sides.
- ☐ I'm breathing slowly and deeply from my abdomen.
- ☐ My heartbeat is calm and composed.
- ☐ I feel a sense of calm and ease in my physical being.
- ☐ I'm able to establish eye contact with those close to me.

MIND:

- ☐ I am able to think with clarity and strategize for the future.
- ☐ I am receptive and curious about others and the world surrounding me.
- ☐ I am engaged in my interests and passions, tapping into my unique creativity.

When our nervous system is acticated, we often behave like a cornered animal. Due to the perceived threat, we go to great lengths to safeguard our survival, often without considering the impact on others. Acknowledging this natural tendency, and recognizing it as inherent human behavior, can help us shed any shame associated with our actions or words during stressful moments. By familiarizing ourselves with the indicators of nervous system dysregulation, we can pinpoint when we're dysregulated, gaining insight into why our behavior or words in relationships can contribute to or intensify interpersonal stress.

Being aware of when we're reacting under stress empowers us to make a deliberate choice to respond differently. Opting for a step back or taking a timeout allows us to remove ourselves from a situation, refraining from interaction until we regain composure and are both capable and willing to engage socially again.

We can all start incorporating mind-body practices, discussed further in the book (and this workbook), to restore our body to a sense of safety. These strategies prove particularly beneficial when we cannot extricate ourselves from an interaction or are unable to leave a stressful environment.

Many of us exhibit recurring trauma bond patterns in our relationships, whether with friends, family, colleagues, or romantic partners. We unconsciously replicate familiar dynamics with others, because our nervous system and subconscious mind are biologically predisposed to reenact the ways we learned to feel secure, valued, or loved during childhood. Until we regulate our nervous system, we perpetuate or strengthen these trauma bonds, regardless of our level of insight or awareness. Fortunately, we all have the capacity to regulate our nervous system.

Notes/insights on the above:

_____

_____

_____

_____

_____

_____

_____

_____

CHAPTER 4: Witnessing Your Conditioned Selves

Your Conditioned Selves Assessment

Review the checklist below and invest some time observing yourself - without passing judgment - in your relationships. Identify the habits that frequently catch your attention, and be aware that you might observe different aspects of yourself in different relationships or as time progresses.

THE CARETAKER:

☐ When I'm in a relationship, I feel a strong inclination to be essential or relied upon.

☐ I'm often very aware of the physical needs of others, and sometimes even attempt to anticipate them before that need arises.

☐ I believe that I experience the greatest love when someone depends on me for care.

THE OVERACHIEVER:

☐ I constantly think about whether others think I'm good enough.

☐ I take satisfaction in being thought of as the top lover/friend/daughter/son, etc.

☐ Normally I'm the one to initiate contact or attend to others, even if it's not returned.

THE UNDERACHIEVER:

☐ I typically steer clear of getting into relationships or have challenges with commitment.

☐ I find it hard to open up or establish emotional connections with others.

☐ I shy away from criticism and situations that might make me feel rejected or abandoned.

THE RESCUER/PROTECTOR:

☐ I find myself drawn to people and connections where the primary emphasis is on the other person.

☐ I feel a sense of love or meaning when someone is emotionally open and relies on me for support.

☐ I often feel strong protective instincts towards those I'm in relationships with, often adopting their point of view even if I don't agree with it.

THE LIFE OF THE PARTY:

- ☐ I frequently steer clear of confrontations in my relationships.
- ☐ I typically avoid discussing my emotions and shy away from conversations that could create discomfort for myself or others.
- ☐ I believe that pretending everything is fine is the most effective approach in a stressful or upsetting situation.

THE YES PERSON:

- ☐ I usually just go with the flow, or prioritize the needs and preferences of my loved ones over my own.
- ☐ In relationships, I often embrace the wants of my friends or loved ones, such as dressing similarly, sharing similar beliefs, engaging in the same hobbies, or adjusting my schedule to fit theirs.
- ☐ I often say yes to activities that others suggest, even if they disrupt my work, rest, or self-care routine.

THE HERO WORSHIPER:

- ☐ When I first meet someone, I have a tendency to be captivated by them and believe they're flawless.
- ☐ I often hide or change aspects of myself that I deem as "shameful" in an attempt to resemble those I idealize.
- ☐ I disregard any imperfections or challenges in my loved ones and typically concentrate solely on their favorable characteristics.

Notes/insights on the above:

_____

_____

_____

_____

_____

_____

Empowerment Pause Exercise

In our learning journey, we've come to understand that our life experiences are influenced by and processed through our conditioned mind. Developing an awareness of our ingrained reactions and behaviors gives us the ability to actively shape and construct the experiences we want, instead of feeling trapped, unsatisfied, or helpless.

This sense of empowerment originates from the prefrontal cortex, a region in our brain responsible for deliberate responses, as well as our capacity to plan, concentrate, control impulses, delay gratification, anticipate outcomes, and regulate emotional responses.

To activate your prefrontal cortex, take a moment to pause before responding to the thoughts, emotions, and urges that arise during your day. This practice allows you to recognize your automatic reactions and creates a space to consciously choose new, more purposeful responses.

The following questions and exercises are designed to encourage exploration of your reactivity and responsiveness.

Recall a time when you responded to an experience, without much thought, and answer the following questions:

What were your physical sensations during and after this burst of reactivity?

_____

_____

_____

_____

How did you emotionally perceive yourself and anyone else involved in this moment of heightened response?

_____

_____

_____

Take a moment to recall an instance when you witnessed someone else's sudden and intense reaction to a situation and consider the following queries:

How did you physically respond during and after observing another person's reactivity?

_____

_____

_____

_____

What were your emotional impressions of both yourself and the individual who was reacting?

_____

_____

_____

_____

Recall a situation when you were able to stay composed in your reactions or decisions, and consider the following:

What were the physical sensations you experience during and after this responsive moment?

_____

_____

_____

_____

How did you emotionally perceive yourself and others in that moment?

_____

_____

_____

_____

Keep in mind that there are no correct answers; the effort to consciously alter ingrained patterns and behaviors starts with this self-exploration, which can be empowering in itself.

When we are consciously aware of our habits, we can make deliberate choices in our relationships rather than consistently reacting to and reproducing old childhood wounds. It allows us to thoughtfully examine how the roles we've assumed since childhood may not be conducive to our authentic selves or our relationships. Integrating our conditioned selves contributes to restoring our sense of safety and security, no matter what is happening externally.

Establishing personal safety and security through daily decisions forms new neural pathways in the brain. With consistent repetition, these pathways can become permanent, and the related habits can become instinctual.

This doesn't imply that you'll never revisit conditioned thoughts, feelings, or reactions or won't feel instinctively drawn back to familiar habits. Becoming aware of your conditioned self or selves provides access to new choices that better align with your true self, your aspirations, and the relationships that genuinely fulfill you. A regulated nervous system facilitates access to these new choices.

Notes/insights on the above:

_____

_____

_____

_____

_____

_____

_____

_____

CHAPTER 7: Unlocking the Power of Your Heart

HRV Self-Assessment

Read the questions below, and choose the responses that most resonate with you.

Do you feel a loss of control, a sense of being flooded, or a tendency to react strongly when you're upset with others?
- ☐ 1. Rarely
- ☐ 2. Occasionally
- ☐ 3. Often

Do you find it challenging to unwind or feel comfortable in the company of others?
- ☐ 1. Rarely
- ☐ 2. Occasionally
- ☐ 3. Often

Do you feel fear, discomfort, or a sense of being unsafe when trying to get close to, or make a connection with others?
- ☐ 1. Rarely
- ☐ 2. Occasionally
- ☐ 3. Often

Are you frequently hesitant, uneasy, or feel insecure about being emotionally open or forming close connections with others?
- ☐ 1. Rarely
- ☐ 2. Occasionally
- ☐ 3. Often

Do you find it hard to open up to love, resisting efforts from others to emotionally connect or express affection toward you?
- ☐ 1. Rarely
- ☐ 2. Occasionally
- ☐ 3. Often

Do you have difficulty unwinding or feeling comfortable in your own company, becoming uneasy during moments of quiet or solitude, such as during meditation or when alone?

- ☐ 1. Rarely
- ☐ 2. Occasionally
- ☐ 3. Often

Tally your responses. The greater your total, the reduced your HRV, and the potential for increased irregularity in your hearbeat. Be compassionate to yourself regardless of your total, and view this as a chance to start changing your physical, mental, and emotional well-being—a transformation that is achievable at any given moment. Regardless of where you stand in your healing process, enhancing HRV and fostering heart coherence through heightened awareness of body and mind can assist you in breaking free from ingrained reactive patterns, discovering calm, and aligning more closely with the messages from your heart.

Notes/insights on the above:

_____

_____

_____

_____

_____

_____

_____

CHAPTER 8: Becoming the Love You Seek

How To Know When Others Are Activated

Engaging in fight, flight, freeze, or shutdown, as well as fawning modes, results in similar observable behaviors. If you can identify when you're having one of these stress responses, you'll likely also be able to tell when someone else is. In the third chapter, we delved into the stress modes linked to the four stress reactions: Eruptor for fight, Distractor for flight, Detacher for freeze or shutdown, and Pleaser for fawn. People may transition into Eruptor, Distractor, Detacher, or Pleaser mode to varying degrees, influenced by the people they're with and the circumstances unfolding around or within them.

In order to tell the current state of someone's nervous system, take a moment to respond to the questions below. If a specific reaction closely aligns with your understanding of your loved one, reflect on the frequency and timing of such responses. This can serve as a guide to anticipate when the person might transition into a state influenced by perceived threats.

Eruptor mode (fight response). An Eruptor directs the majority of their focus outward. This may involve speaking loudly, expressing anger, leaving abruptly, throwing objects, or forcefully closing doors. They may also seek to assert dominance or influence the conversation by overwhelming others or the environment through the volume or content of their speech. While externally appearing composed, there may be an underlying simmering intensity, verging on the brink of eruption. Being in the presence of a person in eruption mode can evoke feelings of fear or a sense of treading carefully, anticipating the next emotional outburst.

How frequently (and at what times) do I sense the possibility of saying or doing something inappropriate, causing an immediate change in my loved one's mood?

_____

_____

_____

_____

_____

How frequently (and at what times) do I perceive that my loved one's anger or distress dominates the emotional atmosphere in the space?

_____

_____

_____

_____

_____

How often (and when) do I hold back from expressing my emotions, convictions, or views because I'm worried about my loved one's potential reaction?

_____

_____

_____

_____

_____

Distractor mode (flight response). A Distractor directs the majority of their focus away from challenging or distressing situations in their surroundings. They might be engrossed in work, maintain an extensive to-do list, excessively rely on technology or television, use substances to numb themselves, or stay consistently occupied.

At times, a person in Distraction mode may embody the role of a highly efficient parent, boss, or partner—someone who efficiently manages everything but remains emotionally distant. When in the company of a person in Distraction mode, you might experience a sense of detachment or being overlooked (unless you're actively participating in the same distraction, such as work, alcohol, household chores, and so forth).

How often is my loved one really 'busy', moving from one activity to the next?

_____

_____

_____

_____

How frequently (and at what times) do I try to connect with my loved one, but find a lack of attention or presence from them during our time together?

_____

_____

_____

_____

How often (and at what times) does my loved one allocate their leisure time to playing video games, browsing social media, or concentrating on another pursuit that anchors their attention externally, diverting it from our interactions?

_____

_____

_____

_____

Detacher mode (freeze or shutdown response). A Detacher directs the majority of their focus inward. They aren't actively expressing or diverting attention; instead, they seem to lack emotion or connection entirely. Identifying this response can be challenging, as a Detacher is often physically present and may even seem involved, but emotionally, they can be empty, distant, or aloof. When in the company of a Detacher, you might sense a remoteness or exclusion, regardless of your actions or words, and may consistently feel rebuffed in your attempts to establish an emotional connection.

How frequently (and at what times) do I catch myself pleading to my loved one to tell me their true thoughts or emotions

_____

_____

_____

_____

How often (and at what times) do I feel very disconnected from my loved one?

_____

_____

_____

_____

How frequently (and at what times) do I experience feelings of rejection or criticism when talking about new interests or experiences to my loved one?

_____

_____

_____

_____

Pleaser mode (fawn response). A Pleaser directs a significant portion of their attention towards the happiness of others. They consistently anticipate the desires of those around them, strive to fulfill others' needs, engage in acts of service, or consciously steer clear of conflicts. A Pleaser often struggles to articulate their own desires and regularly defers to the opinions of others. Being in the company of a Pleaser may evoke feelings of being overwhelmed, suffocated on an emotional level, or resentful.

How often (and at what times) do I observe my loved one engaging in activities just because someone else said to do so?

_____

_____

_____

_____

_____

How often (and when) does my loved one approach me for something (validation, emotional assistance, comforting connection), and how often do I feel at ease or secure doing the same with my loved one?

_____

_____

_____

_____

_____

How frequently (and at what times) do I notice that my loved one speaks or acts to 'keep the peace' or please others, leading to increased conflict in the long term?

_____

_____

_____

_____

Recognizing when our loved ones are emotionally dysregulated helps us guide them back to a sense of security using the co-regulation techniques provided. This approach also helps separate their actions from the personal - understanding that their responses stem from a perceived sense of insecurity rather than a direct reaction to us.

Notes/insights on the above:

_____

_____

_____

_____

_____

_____

_____

_____

_____

CHAPTER 9: Empowering Your Relationships

Empowerment Consciousness Self-Exploration: Journal Prompts

Use these questions to pinpoint areas where you feel empowerment and interdependence in your relationships, as well as areas where there's room for enhancing relational empowerment and interdependence. Reflect on each of your relationships, noting your thoughts and emotions below.

What emotions come up when I'm around this person? How do I feel before and after our interactions?

_____

_____

_____

_____

_____

What areas do I like about this person? Conversely, what do I dislike or find concerning?

_____

_____

_____

_____

_____

Do they communicate honestly and consistently, doing what they say they're going to do? Alternatively, do they exhibit dishonesty and inconsistency, saying one thing and doing another?

_____

_____

_____

_____

Is there room in our relationship for emotional openness and alignment? In other words, are my feelings acknowledged and understood?

_____

_____

_____

_____

Do they pay attention to requests and respect the boundaries I choose to set?

_____

_____

_____

_____

Do they explicitly express their needs?

_____

_____

_____

Are they aware of and accountable for their roles and emotions in the relationship?

_____

_____

_____

Do we share common goals, and do our values match?

_____

_____

_____

Am I open to this type of relationship right now?

_____

_____

_____

Does our relationship feel healthy, and is it a path I want to sustain as is? What needs to changea about our relationship dynamic, for me to want to continue, and for it to be healthy?

_____

_____

_____

_____

_____

It's absolutely fine if you're uneasy or disheartened by some answers to these questions. Consider your answers as a chance or a starting point to recognize and clarify areas you'd like to address. Identifying what isn't working can often guide you toward what will work, even if it involves changing the dynamics of your current relationship or exploring uncharted territory on your own. Keep in mind that ending a relationship when it no longer aligns with your goals, or when you've reached a sense of completion is different from leaving in search of something better, a path many, including the author (she notes), have taken before. Be patient, allowing yourself time and space to mourn any changes or losses in your relationships, even those you've initiated.

While considering your present situation or starting new relationships, persist in granting yourself kindness and understanding. Keep in mind that everyone is evolving, making strides as best they can. Your progress so far is a remarkable indication of your determination and dedication for positive change in yourself, and your connections.

Notes/insights on the above:

_____

_____

_____

_____

_____

CHAPTER 10: Reconnecting with the Collective

Social Coherence Checklist

Use this checklist to evaluate your existing level of social coherence. Be honest and impartial in your self-assessment. Keep in mind that getting what we want starts with acknowledging our current reality. Review the statements below and indicate the response(s) that most closely align with your situation.

- ☐ Im' aware of my emotions during and after consuming specific content, such as TV shows, podcasts, and social media.
- ☐ I can recognize the relationships, situations, or experiences that bring about a sense of lightness, hopefulness, and expansiveness or openness.
- ☐ I can pinpoint the relationships, situations, or experiences that make me feel insecure, heavy, anxious, concerned, restricted, or uneasy.
- ☐ I can acknowledge when I'm overwhelmed and can seek or accept support.
- ☐ I experience a secure connection with those in my surroundings and can genuinely express myself to them.
- ☐ I can take into account both my individual needs and those of the group or broader community.
- ☐ I know which activities bring me enjoyment.
- ☐ I am aware of my values and regularly strive to embody them and work towards goals in my relationships.
- ☐ I am aware of what inspires me and uplifts me.
- ☐ I engage in open and active communication with others, creating a calm exchange of thoughts and emotions.
- ☐ I address conflicts by seeking to understand the lived experiences and perspectives of others.
- ☐ I not only acknowledge my own personal achievements, but also celebrate the successes of those around me.

The greater number of statements you marked, the higher the probability that you are progressing towards social cohesion and capable of impacting the experiences of those around you. As you proceed on your journey, you can return to this checklist as a means to observe and recognize your growth.

Notes/insights on the above:

_____

_____

_____

_____

_____

_____

_____

_____

_____

You made it!
You've completed the workbook.

Claim your free bonus

There's a free bonus waiting for you as thanks for picking up this workbook. We think you'll like it. Inside, you'll find a list of the most impactful self development books from this year, including:

- Top books for self-growth and mindfulness
- Top books for financial growth
- Top books for relationships (including yourself)
- Top books for productivity and "Getting Things Done"

We hope they provide a little inspiration for you - and perhaps some new discoveries.

To get your free bonus, scan the QR code below or visit BigActionBooks.com/bonus.

Scan to get your free bonus

Would you help us with a review?

If you enjoyed the workbook, we'd be so grateful you could help us out by leaving a review on Amazon (even a super short one!). Reviews help us so much - in spreading the word, in helping others decide if the workbook is right for them, and as feedback for our team.

If you'd like to give us any suggestions, need help with something, or to find more workbooks for other self-development books, please visit us at BigActionBooks.com.

Thank you

Thank you so much for picking up the Workbook for Dr. Nicole LePera's *How to Be the Love You Seek*. We really hope you enjoyed it, and that it helped you practise the lessons in everyday life.

Thanks again,
The Big Action Books team

 BIG ACTION BOOKS

Notes

Notes

_____

_____

_____

_____

_____

_____

_____

_____

_____

_____

_____

_____

_____

_____

_____

Notes

Notes

Notes

Notes

Notes

Notes

Made in United States
Troutdale, OR
12/17/2024

26568790R00038